Life on a Farm

Written by Margie Burton, Cathy French, and Tammy Jones

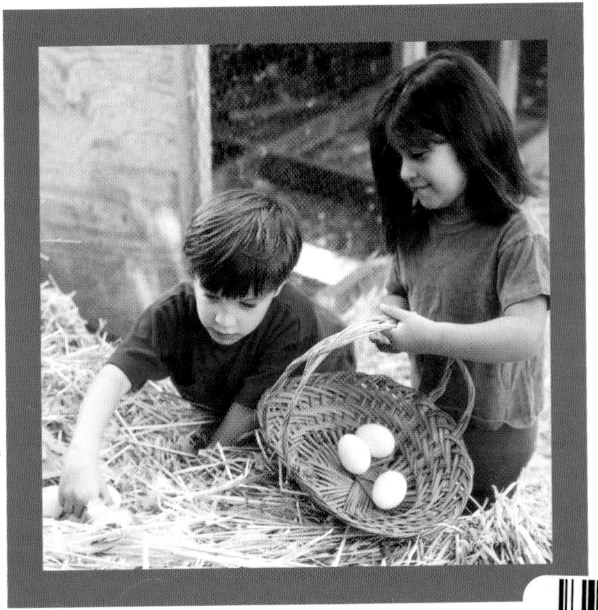

I am milking.

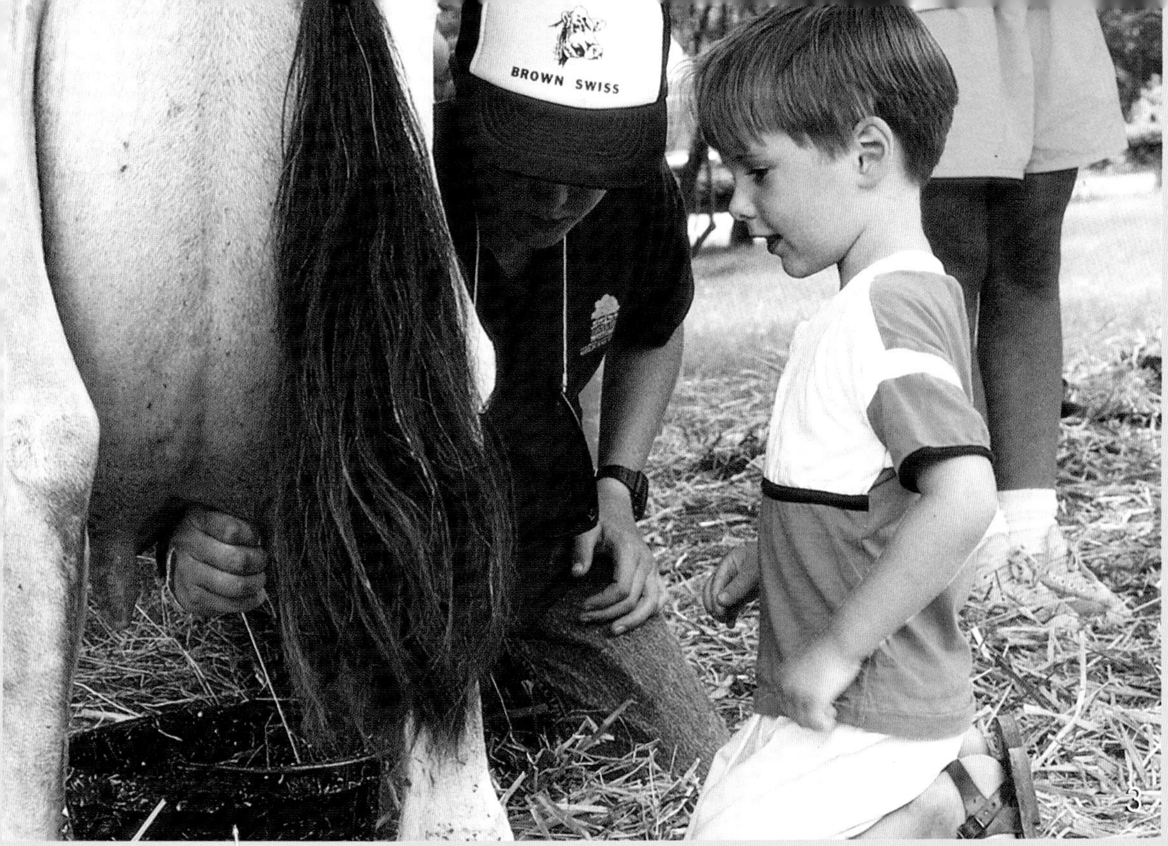
BROWN SWISS

I am driving.

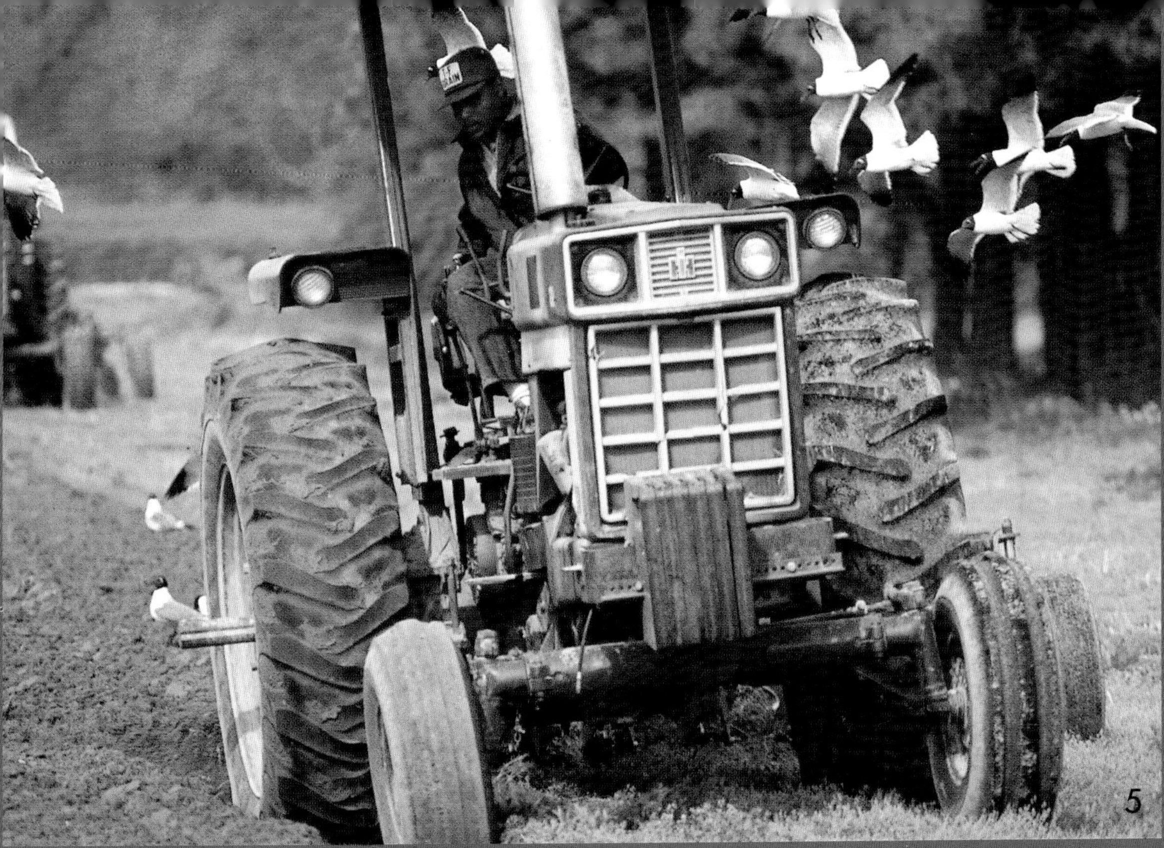

I am riding.

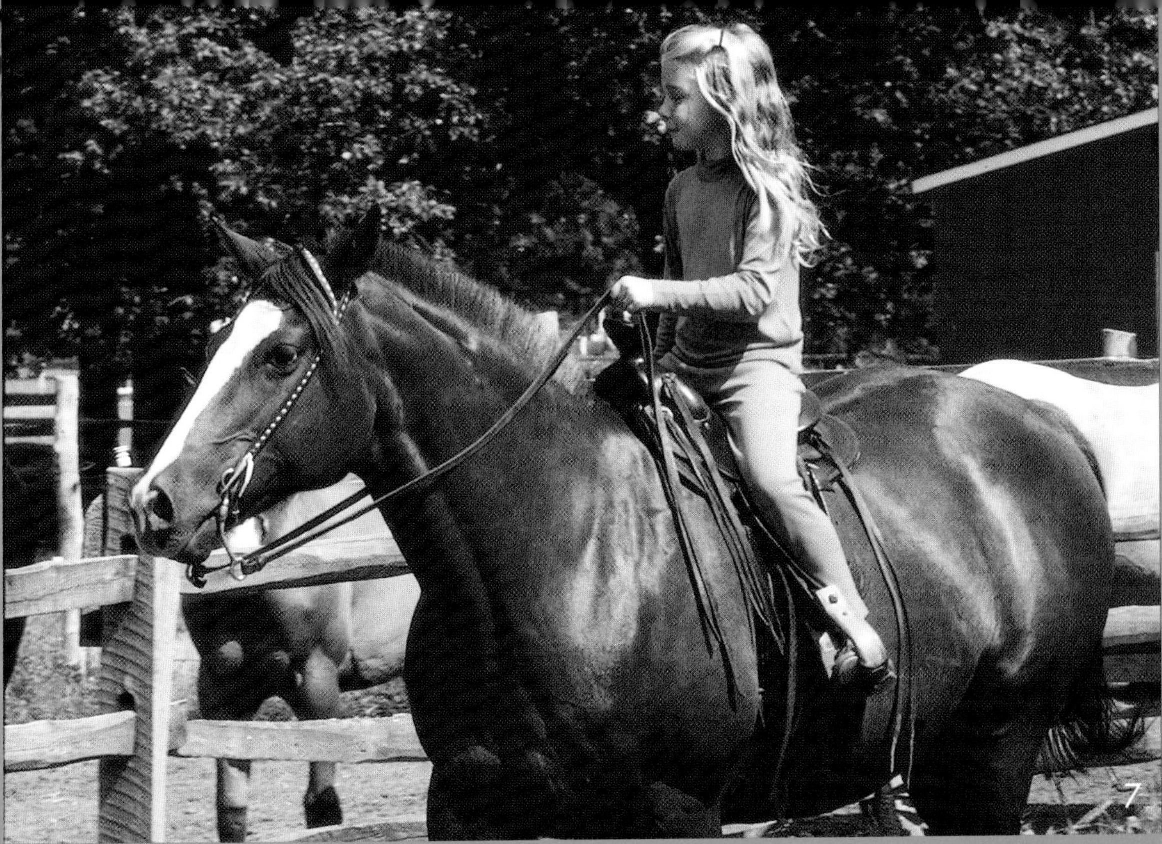

I am picking.

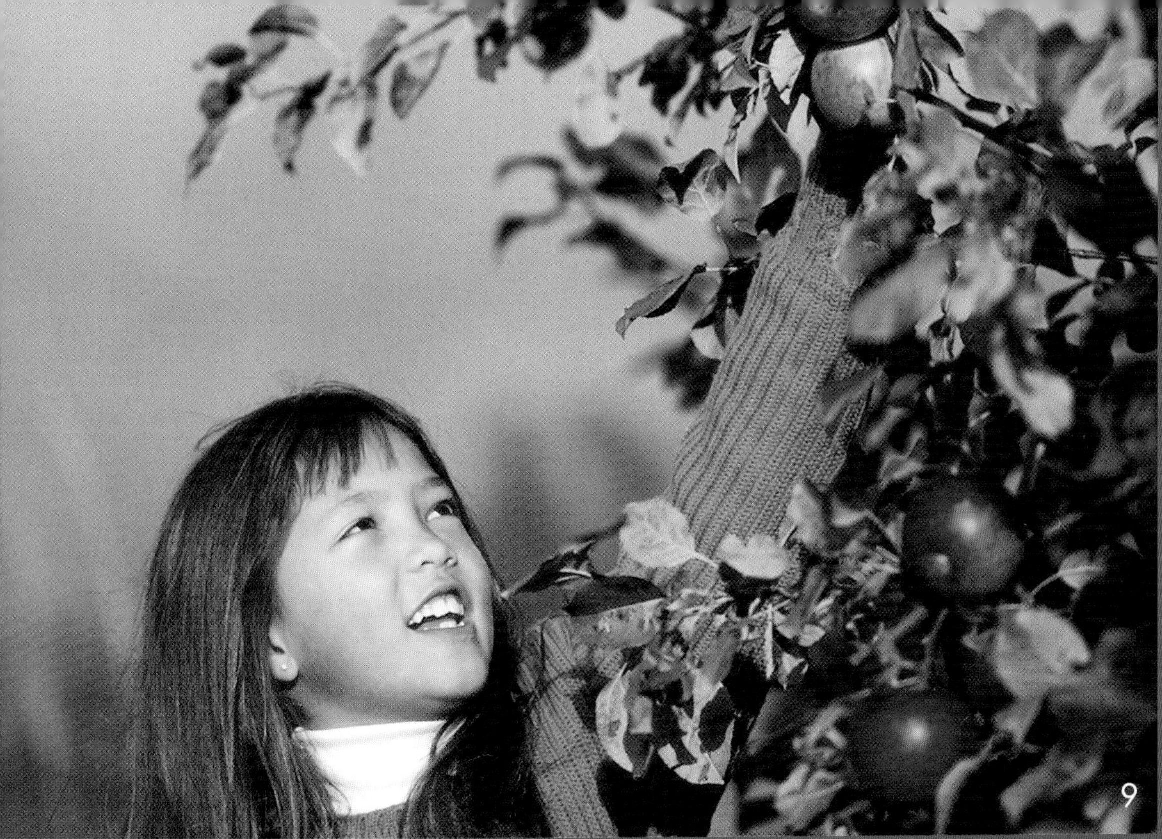

I am digging.

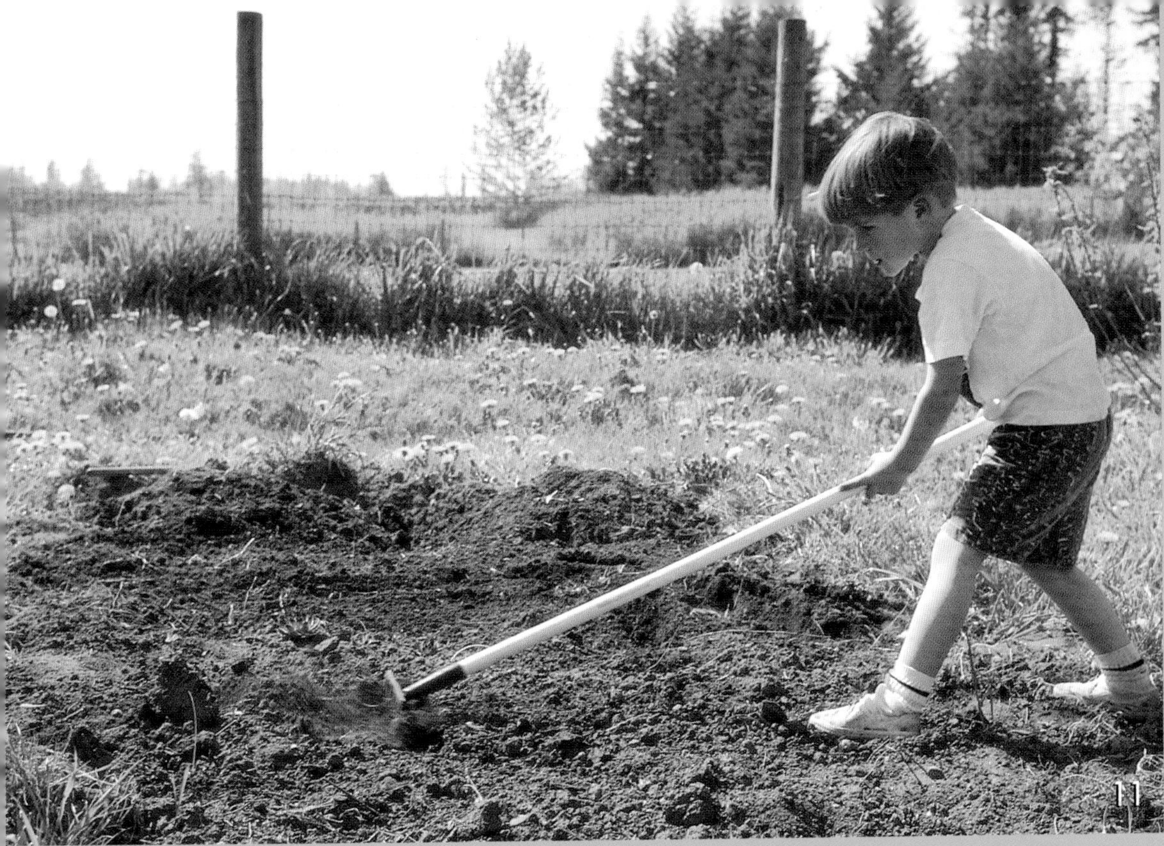

I am sawing.

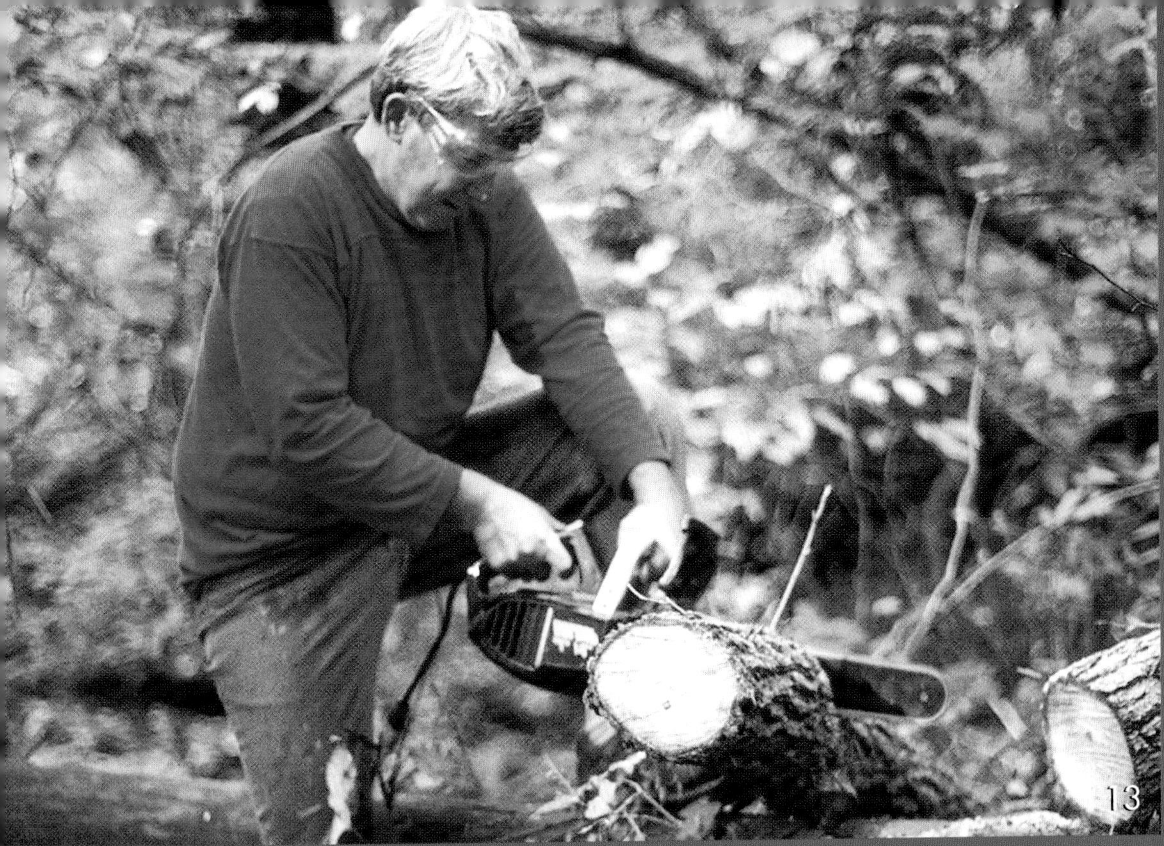

I am feeding.

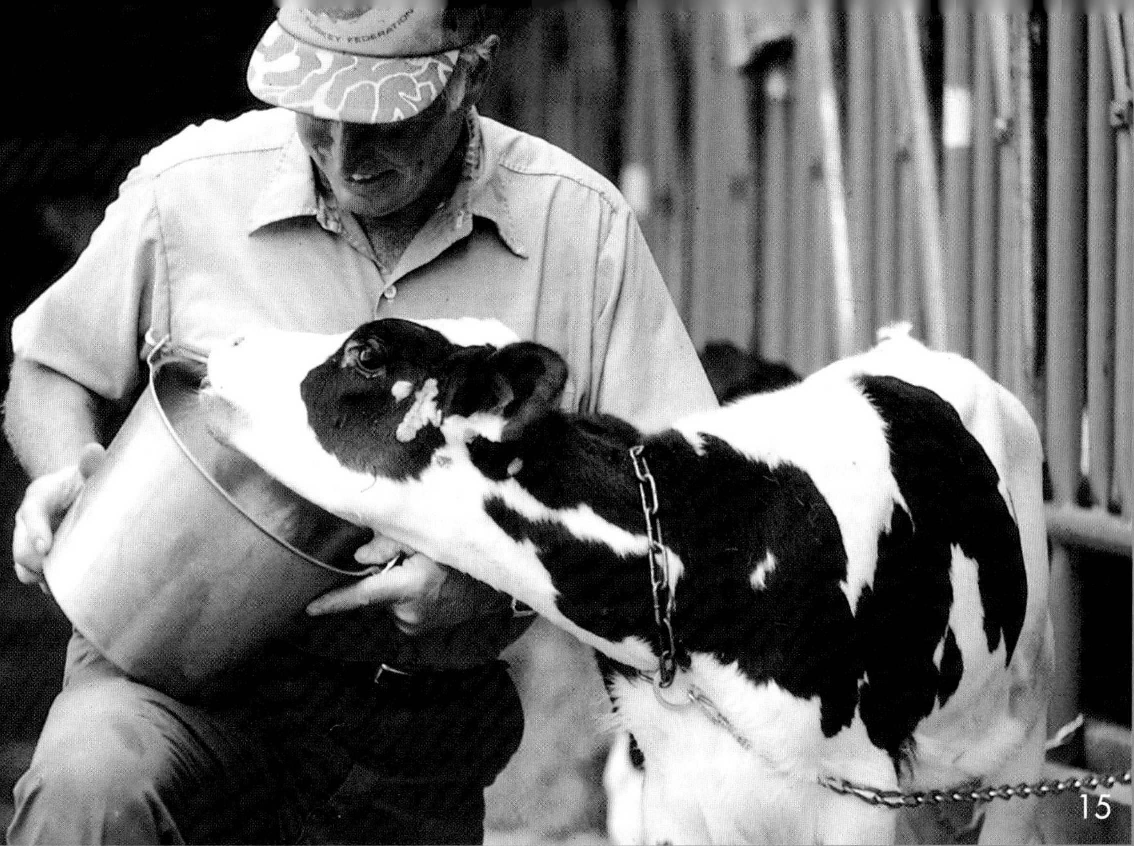
FEDERATION

I am cooking.

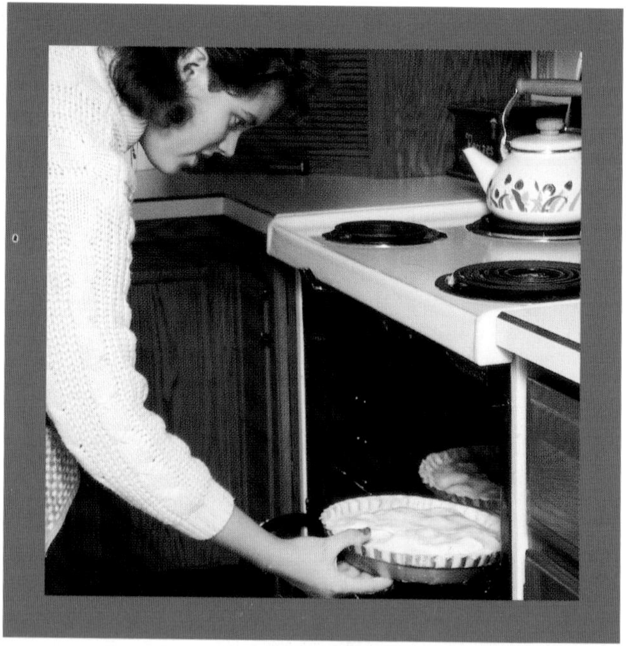